Chico Hermano
And
Lyrics For Poetic Mutts

Poems

Billy Townes

"I fear no man but God, but then again fear is just a concept created to make us bow down to absent landlords and swine alike."
\- Lee Weller

(Untitled)

What motive of brotherhood
So shrill
In laughter
The eternal comedy of it all plays aloud
Thumping really
And I laugh in the general direction of this misfortune
Such circumstances employ the humorous
In the depths and pattern we vibrate
At hard won effort holding back
What unfortunate a fool
At leagues with victor
The chromosomal shareholders they are
Now one has and hits lead off
The method to gain the edge

In consolation
He finds the fiscal reward
Minute after previous withdrawal
That in his hands would put more the burden
Nearly multiplying a prize
But no
So small it is
With regards to comparison
Nearly invisible
His parallel makes guttural noise
Throwing the verbal compassion in support
Support
Support
The type unneeded
What would reach the benefit
Well let me see
Some Reaganomical power plays hit the mind
Those golden hypotheticals
It all flows from mountains
Initially that is
We only need to wait for the thaw
Once dams and levees collapse
Some stimulants might just rain down
Though the slow speed is probable
Past examples always get a bit blurry on sight
We may just need a pass
I've heard funds are a word of use

The hedge variety seems bankable

Harsh Growl in Smooth Stone

And just how would Vienna speaks
Would its floors and walls collapse
Fall into open earth jaws
Harsh words out flying directionless
Eating soft footed passers
Is that how?

What mystic nonsense
Holding no sense
Vienna hasn't the gruesome teeth
No you can't find that sort of thing
Not this side of cold waters

These quarter east locales
Partially northern
Have old enough roots to know better
The quick hand-fall of them all
Black and blue from old encounters
Turned to new mindsets
Some get all spiritual about it
Which is fine in few
Those in sight have quieted
Introspective looks upon their
Well no face
Upon their
Whatever holds that anthropomorphic quality
I don't know
I in honesty can't find
Why would I search beyond these walls
Attempt to change the streets into what they aren't meant to be

Nickel Wound Bronze

Sing that sweet music
On key with syncopation
Create some innate rhythm
You are modulating
You are sustained
You are maple
Imported woods
You are Hendrix
Healey
At a touch
Early instances
You burn fingers in metallic fire
Change the sheer fabric of skin
Speeds will rip and tear away
In pain pain hard pain
But what a sickly sweet drug
Hitting all highways at once
A brain so exhilarated
It melts
Drains out the ears
Leave a bucket at side for such events
I will repeat until the tools fall off

I'm Told They're Called Synapses

When days fall past like this
We have little to do but think
All other flesh spurns to concrete
So unmoving
Only that minor electricity's free to flow
As neck stiffs to plaster
That shoddy grey rattles back back and forth and forth
If you stand in the wind
The bounce and sensation becomes apparent

Results are shipped in odd shapes
Conforming to others in meer fleeting coincidence
Rotten poetique blasts through plugged ears
Mental movements
Before watching eyes
All rolled
Cramped to one
To only

I think of Dante after time
All his verse
The meaning within
That power uponn power
Impression of the genius hand
How though
His words are not here
Have they ever been
No
So hard to cross water
Time and
And what exactly is the word
A mind in such atmosphere will never answer
Phantom speed leave those loose ends
Now that head has pieces
Once that string ends you'll have nothing
Damned frustration and all
I really question that monster's associates
Evil agent
Having infected the body
Shaves its understanding low
Some devil ordering for enjoyment

Foul
Foul cur organ
Better without in truth
Quick cut removal
Works for so many
Even minus procedure
And look at new profession
Hell

If Horror Had the Keys

How a being can sleep
Never lifting limb
Yet can stare with glaring eyes
A beast of a gargoyle
With each breath it gains teeth
Growing to saber cat
Proportionately to my knowledge
Teeth piercing grey fibre
Too carefree
What detrimental evolution
Cementing it likewise
Cruel
Horrifying

And I call in control for forced removal
One and forty five
Never never never
I will never stand to be scammed as such
Not by you
Never
I have drastic resorts
And flammable materials at hand
It will never beat such attrition
Such heat

(Untitled)

Turn back before they ask
Before those fools gain the energy to tell
Tell they will
On and on
Each forceful remark forcing removal
Removal of what was
What would have been planned
Every plan
Without the grace of discrimination
A simple burn
Allowed to spread to all edges
Step aside a moment early
Anticipating their will
Act on that slightest twitch
And move in that occasion of silence
It can be the only way
It should be
Whether it will
Lies on you
You fool
So act
Or not

Puppets Crawl and Critics Bawl

Quality in reality bows to the variety
All of those nearly infinite factors
Yet experience stands atop the pile
Over corpses and husks
Beaming in its utter importance
Without
What could there be
Cutouts
Shadow puppets of a portrayal
Painted in those appealing colours
Presented with quick movements in distraction
The mass grave will bow to its awe
Blinded by that first layer
Seeing the real layer with a few sure steps
But too late
All will hail it by name
MIsnomer
Misnomer in hell
And quality will distort and
Distort and
Distort and become real

Floorboard Opus #13

Doris Day runs through dead wonderlands
While the crown prince
The scum he is
Takes it in from the sidelines
At height
Round each corner
That flash of the old celebrated
Her tracks
The ripples in the wall

What am I supposed to make of this
Jumbled mess of a mess
Can I really run a string through
Discover what should be at the heart
When letting a thing sit
Such as now
Presents itself as so widely prefered

And if Sophia Loren were to walk down
On hers and borrowed ankles
Where would it play in line with the whole
It would all change
So naturally beyond nature
Changing to a state unfit for myself
The doomed saviour would have to crawl in
Taking reigns in muddened hands
Finding where
In hell
It all belongs

That Doomed Mind

In the noted heat
I heard the wise poem of Rome
Long before Rome had stone
As I lay afterwards
I felt the future's past crawl near
But not now
These eyes couldn't stand it
It's taking everything involuntary to hold the glue
So Jack I push my pen
To the unfortunate death of it's balled point
Attempting only to speak a dead tongue
For I cannot now
Though I will not hold this for time
Bear that damned earth old wall
Well
Let me see what my hands can kill
I am driven to squeeze some creativity out
Grind it into a powder
Gorge myself on those mineralized
Mineralized
The world's gone sour again dammit
Back to that bare blackboard
You see Jack
The words are all backwards and non-existent
Hence the weeks
Dry weeks
Dead weeks
Without hen to hail
Or stone to throw
I don't know how you lived
There is the slight shrieking reality
Pitiful isn't it
That you too were doomed to these valleys
Were you Jack?
Don't answer
I'd rather be slave to my assumptions
It helps to dull the senses
And hell
If we can find the right level
Dull and dull and dull and dull
We might just fly high and out
Then I'll have something to say

Something I can't prepare to comprehend
Then you'll hear it
Which would be impressive Jack
Quite impressive

Bastards the All

Are you the one that finds virtue in malevolence
Or
Do you live in a code of stone
You have created these choices
If you wish to force others
The personal choice must be made
Would you rather bring odd chaos upon the world?
Upon us all?
You look of sly material
But the facilities aren't there
I would be taken if by some gesture
Prior groundwork had been planned
It just isn't in you
What is on that matter?
Such a husking shell
You shake and hear rattles
The odd end falls out
Finding its avenue to ground

Of use
If you own the resource
Or are willing to take it
Then in sense
A lot could be accomplished
Whether pushing in a proper direction
I would have to doubt
I have seen your records
And at infinitum
It circles
We will see it again again again
I am willing to wager
And what a sour bet
Misfortune makes for an uneasy game

In Theory

You'll always hear of those far off fools
The ones who see old celluloid
Take it a bit too close to heart
Seeing a world of panelled colour
As nothing but the light playing tricks
Only only images
Electric paintings gone mad
Fools fools the lot of them
They cannot see the windows before them
Looking out at the world once our own
Stills and names
Not else
For all that matters is the mind first imagined
Of course
All that matters is what we can grasp from it
Right
What is ripe for harvest
I have cried fool once
More than once
I shall cry it again
my threat will bleed from such repetition
And what will they learn
Nothing
As has been their pattern
There are some who seem incapable

Caroline's Tongue

Monsieur
I must request your removal
Immediately if possible
After my own thorough consideration
I have become convinced of a beloved alternative
With so much imprisoned potential
Just beyond that door of theoretics
Wait can I spell theoretics
It seems misplaced
Maybe the pluralization is off
As is it's a bit wicked
Takes control of that line
Oh no but it should
Hence the whole meaning
Right?
No but those letters have no meaning
Only my mind holds that
As far as I can believe
At least
Shit
What track was I on
Let's give a moment's pause
I'll find the right vowels somewhere
Just over there isn't it?
Ah yes
You can see the line exactly
Where it all trailed off
I'm sending it in for a fix
We'll get the experts in on this one
Pick up on the initial

No Hand to Hold

You always speak of this hope
Revered and holy
In your eyes it comes falling
Down from blue skies
Never gray
Gently finding our hands
And guiding us forward
But my eyes must have cracks
As I cannot see your standards
my windows gained a glaze
From which that wayward hope could not be viewed

Oh you must turn around
In your words
I've been searching those wrong corners
If so then tell me
Where is that hope
That sprouts from the ground like ripened weeds
Where is that hope
THat lays around awaiting its daily use
Always waiting
Always waiting
You are always waiting
For that hopeful sky to fall at such speeds
To land graceful at your lap
Well now I am the one who screams fool

Disbelieving that hopeful surplus
I move through all streets
Through winds
Through rain
Creating all that I need for myself
KNowing when to close my ears
Belittling those lackadaisical words at the source

Preparing for a New Age

And we all get too much credit
We do we do
The far chosen saviours
Aren't we?
Oh what a dream
So self importantly themed and planned
Yes the steps we make lay stone
But what a stone crumbles
Even below strong shoes
That bowl upstairs wouldn't see
Not till it hits the rubble
But oh oh well
I cannot hold these mad thoughts forever
In cases as such
A fool must accept the way the world turns
Must accept his own crowd
The vague vague crowd that is little but a name
A name that shutters in my dry threat
So dry after all air has been removed
Inflating those heads
Heads heads heads heads heads
I will throw sharp objects through their current
Take them out at the neck
What a laugh as they float and fall
Losing no use
Remaining useless

April 14th

Barely bleached
It flies down streets
In face of hard rain
When in all minds the sun should shine
Street lights collapse in shadow
Fall overtop
Slowing it all to a crawl
Before melting away
Leaving clouds in the air
Dissolving
Accumulating in throats
Scraping lining while blood flows

And as the mobile freeze
We
The onlookers
Fear that which hides in close corners
It creeps through our walls
Barges in if given leeway
Without procedures to fallback
It takes us all
Snaps us upright

But what change will come in time
How can we look back
Behold this past as such
Rosey eyes ablaze and all
my bones will shake blue
Yet the mind sees gold on screen
With tints and wedges
Until our hills rise sideways once more
And our mind's eye freezes over

I Know Many Like This

Oh ho Picasso
What and odd mind you've made
Dismantle what they believe
Reassemble
Build what you imagine
Picture the world of your hand
The uncontrolled mannequin man of fame
Viewed like adonis
Allowed to exist
As no one else has
Let them pay you in paper
Or walls blank
Repay their patience in action

Now they must be taught
Teach them possibilities
Show movements against curves
Or show no movement at all
Display interpretations of nonexistence
Rewrite your end result
Then dance upon it

Those hands that drop creations
Those beings with imagined wit
You will only allow them the grace
Why of course only they would accept it
So that is your grand trick
Which repeats to infinity
The sly bastard you are
This is where my respect will lie

I'd Rather Become a FishMonger

Nic Wray
Nic Wray
I know all that you wanted to tell
All that needed to be known
But as you know my honouree
Instinct prevails in the mind
A man who can cultivate masters
Can hold strong the word of a god
Now Nic Wray
Nic Wray
September did you well
Did it?
I'm partial to the prior months
When a cold drink becomes groundwater
As authors know
A drink can shift
While the stooges destroy

Now monsieur let me qualify
I'm no yacht club maitre de
Though I know my way around a manhattan
Trust me as I speak
I have read enough to understand
I have learned to keep my ears like concrete
One must inject nothing
Throw away all anchors
It will all become clear
It will all become simple
If done correctly
But correctly is a loose word
With odd moving letters
Letters that flip two sides with a twist
So disregard that stipulation

A man with one eye
Whether present or not
Taught me this lesson
Threw me the rope
Allowing me to pull when I saw fit
With this rope I caught life
Surrounded everything with meaning
Now rope is an ancient tool

That can always be lengthened
All it needs is an eye
Equal in age
And a pencient for the needless

Oh So Young… Oh So Young…

Zobruthe Natalia
I saw you at twenty four
I saw you much earlier
When I had other eyes
Old models
You had other arms
We traded legs
Boxcars send white roses
Cadillacs in lime green
Your gift took two forms
One beat southward
The other is something that gypsies speak of

Zobruthe Natalia
Rails to the heart of it all
Chasing our cat tails

Zobruthe Natalia
Mein Orson was a father
Held high hands above
Then on and on and on
To the company of the maistro

Zobruthe Natalia
Names will be thrown around
And oh how it will continue
They will take you to coasts
Drag your feet to the front
Shoot you past streetlights at sundown
As they will someday
To us all
To us all

Feline

Now watch as the cat shoots forward
Far spread with its iron claw
Sprawling over wind and water

Has it ever found solace
Will it know the grace upon it
Can a being of such thought
Harboring such malice
Exist at all
Is it natural
Is it our own product
Our own intelligent creation

How can it be
That a creature like this
Moves in such ways
Never failing
Always landing

I'm partial to others
Personally more acceptable
Those who bring along no harm
However unintentional

Advice From Death Himself or Some Radical Mosaic Figure Who Paraded by the Window at an Altogether too Early Hour of the Morning

Jean mon frere
You'll find out soon
The ride always comes to an end
It's the rule
We can't just have free roamers
We'd have nothing for the path ahead
And listen brother
The path ahead matters more than the trail behind

Let's keep our eyes front for now
I've got mine peeled
Anchored more or less
Now let's shift yours likewise
We'll move as one today

Oh now
This is what I'm talking about
Watch 'em shuffle in
Trudge like cattle in a mule train
It's a clear example
They aren't looking for our target
But why would they?
It does not belong to them
As we are blind to their motives
They own our negative
What a crazy thought eh?
Move on now
We've got a lot more to cover
And my voice is getting hoarse

Heatwave

It's a nervous heat
The kind that leaves your hands in burning ice
Boiling most
My nose melts away
Gifting my face a new void
A convenient cavern
Perfect for hidden hideaways
The door combusts on queue
And the house falls to pieces
Revealing the new kingdom
Shelter of the calming peaceful mantra
It calls to the lake dwellers
With high-top-speakers
Blasting new chic vibrations
If they can make it past the river
Of molten rock and
Oh what else could it be
Any variety really
It all blends together eventually
Then it passes through
Shakes away the shakes
To build a monolith towering high
Which casts shadows
Long and
Damn not this again
Long and cyclical
That cools my heads
Cool enough to cross the river
And reach the far banks

Early Morning

The robin takes a branch
Sings kala kala kala
Does two half steps
And flies east

The crow hangs on high wires
Laughs at all below
Spots the coming crowd
Preaches his feathered knowledge

The hound lays beneath the sun
Claiming warmth as its own
Eyeing its land
Instilling its dominance

The cat wanders off to the side
Believing its imagined invisibility
It steps to unfamiliar sounds
And sneaks off for a better view

The family trudges in line
Coughing up sludge
Never looking forward
They miss what all can see

Shack Alack Black

Shack alack black
With a hint of blue spruce
The sky falls above my head
As the streets flee from my steps
Now I soar on rough terrain
A shifting landscape in front
Time sends my older self onward
While history cradles my youth

Now shush your words harshly
Scream a soft tone
Put your shoes on with moxie
Moxie moxie moxie
Never let it be heard by him
For he shall steal what you hold
In your arms and mind
He'll advertise
Shell it out to the crowd at half price
Then it will lose all meaning
And your sweat will fall on useless sleeves

So I will live in the heat
Stare into the bright abyss
And await the inevitable
The walls will crumble
The carpet will stain
Calls will go answered
But ignored
The rooms will ring high pitched
Ing ing ing ing ing ing ing
I will chase them into a field
And release them to the wild

The Tower of Jeremiah

Art is nonsensical
An entity which by its nature deflects definition
The hopeless spend years
Even lifetimes
Pointlessly pondering over limited labels
Art is supposedly interconnected with humanity
We suckle upon it for life
Claims have been made
With little concrete support
That in its absence time would fail
Hard headed mongrels use it as a defense
Encasing their self obsessed opus-es from the eyes of non-believers
Art is non necessary
In the absence of colour
The rose lives on
The eyes become accustomed to gray
That may be an ill informed statement
So let me rephrase
Artists
As individuals
Are not the eternal
Poets could cease to exist tomorrow
Some other group of heretics would take their place
Musicians are doomed
Their craft is too natural for them to monopolize
Rhythm is widespread in nature
Melody predates the best by fortnights
A chef will put the hardest fight
Some say their work is essential
That it sustains
While chefs are the only carriers of that truth
A cornucopia of white shirts
With eyes for some outer soul
Have gifted me with life for most of my knowing time
A respectful
No nonsense air surrounds them
A shredding tightrope at their feet
Fear of the eventual alleyway beating
The inspiration that drives a genius to madness
Shows the genius of a madman
Most will never come close to experiencing the tantrum
Therefore

We will never understand art
The incomprehensible ideal
So the universe is happy
Revelling in our continued ignorance

A Title for a No One but Myself

If I had to guess
I dream by three day periods
Approximately
What entails is rarely if ever clear
Fleeting glimpses are presented in full feature form
Contorting time towards the unrecognizable
Yet they never leave clear trails
Always miraculously escaping
Residing beyond my search radius
Still images stay behind occasionally
The footprint of some larger nonsensical abstract
In enough time it may reveal one act
But the grander play is gone

I have dreamt of girls
Ghouls
And guitars
Simultaneously at times
Heads say these mental mirages own meaning
Maybe they do
But I'm not one to go full Freudian
Hell if you want to be the one to take a crack at this skull
All power to you
You'll get nowhere at a slow pace
But you'll get your hours in
So who can complain
I'm all for wasting time

Monsieur

To my compatriot on far coasts
From the high hills
Whose eyes have seen more than is cared to calculate
These streets are calling to you mon ami
For weeks at high volume
I speak personally when I say I echoe their effects
But simultaneously I cannot come to agreement
You wouldn't recognize these walls
The faces so familiar
Yet untrustworthy
My dear Jean-Luc
This is such a confusing time
I can no longer say anything with certainty
It's starting to get to my head
And my bones are beginning to ache
Let's just say that I as an individual
And the crowd of like minded delinquents
Request your input
As well as your sympathy
Some sense needs to be made
Or at least convincingly fabricated
Whether you are the one to do it cannot be said
Not yet
We'll have to leave it to chance

Mourning (Gulag Lovers In Space and Time)

I'm a hound in the gutter
No hands
No eyes
I believe in what I hear
But so troubled I am to listen
The falling water is ice cold
And my shroud become snow
My feet
Numb
Run off
Leaving the flesh assortment behind
The sun rises past rackets
Bringing aches pains scrapes and cuts
Slow dribble of life
Slow to river
Mean river
River never to cross
Despite visual nonsense
Clarity comes creeping
What a face
What a world
Uncapturable
Far away from my common comprehension
Too long these floodgates will be open
No street breaching sight for time
Won't match a gaze
There are no hounds in that slime
Only mice
Afraid of owls
Poor fools
No true vision or touch
No taste for cold street corners
Or mangy gutter holylands

The Independent Screwball Press with Regards to the Energy of the Scene

We are allowed a fleeting opportunity
Freedom beyond our self imposed borders
The likes of which few before have seen
We have final cut
No need for final editions

There is no foreseeable circumstance
No single one
To which this could benefit us in anyway
This means nothing of course
Any beneficial quality would hamper the mood
Demoralize the whole lot
Meaning is unnecessary
We only need instinct
To blindly march forward
Despite harsh rebellion
And scream at the top of our lungs
Pointless prose which will fall
Exclusively
On voluntary deaf ears

Whether the deeper understanding is comprehended
Remains up in the air
Flying up there with our willingness
An element which remains elusive
To all but the worst of us
Gravity has no control over it
So some outside assistance is needed

Head Games/Morgan Bridge Ferry

Amnesia
A strange concept
Some have it forced upon them
An unnatural byproduct
Runoff from pseudoscience catastrophes

A man
Let's say a troubadour
Stricken with the sickness
Would have nothing but the future
Only the future
No past to wax nostalgic
No hazy visions of far off memories
Only that which no man can predict
Relying solely on the future
The eternal enigma
Shifts the geometric soul
Beyond recognizable measures
Morph and bend a creature
Leave nothing behind

If it was on demand
I may just be a repeat customer
Selectively of course
No need for complete reset
I just need to vacate the filler

Blue
Nothing but
Complete and all encompassing
So blue it changes
Dark purple
Low magenta
Back again
I no longer need to see all aspects
Use memory to visualize
Hear it moving like a wave
Almost as if it was intentional
Who knows what was going on at the time
Joni's mind the subject
Should I ever know
I feel it speaks for itself
Hell
Could I describe it
my mind
Preoccupied
No words will form
Not words of my own
Sit back
Relax
A moment as such becomes hard to come by

Beat in the Pit

Those stone masons are a crafty bunch
They've got webs from here to burghs
From the Maldives to Golden States
They're here
They're there
They lurk
They scheme
Eyeing the prize at all times
You scratch an ear
Cough a tone
At the sudden you're draped i robes and sigels
You lock eyes with the wrong fool
The next thing you know there's sack over head
You're caught going ninety
Chanting preachers at lefts and rights
Scrolls and candles
Very least
I appreciate the scents
What is that
Lemon tequila beachtime sunrise
Not my choice
It fits the whole dark cult facade
The drapes are garish
Silk or suede
Tarp more like it
They went persian with the rug I see
Quite the patchwork
Good to know they only shell out for class
I'm really aligning with the atmosphere
Get a minibar
Throw pillows
We could get a real baroque movement here

Cosmic Debris

Cosmic as a descriptor
Plunging through
Reverberating with wicked mumbo jumbo
Back and forth until the energy runs dry
A sort of alternative electricity
Power that can change
Minds
Men
All that it touches turns
To what?
Who knows
It is far beyond us
We're not gonna catch unless we kick into overdrive
Ah but the clinical cosmos begins to drip
Sails far
Far away
Far gone from its determined masses
It leaves us with little
Mean pride
And a hint at the possibilities
Goes on to another plane
Defying existence
Molding a new reality
It leaves a trail
That few can decipher
Not meant to be understood
Not by us
Or anyone
For it is cosmic
And does as it sees fit

Fever

Living in a world of nothing but light
Boiling in my own skin
Organs bursting
One and another
The liver calms to save a few souls
Kidneys come 'round
Even the score
I need ice water
I need air
Whatever works
And soon
Some padres are coming to gouge out eyes
I can't cancel again
I'll have to follow the old yogi
What he preached
Forward
Backward
Move beyond my natural boundaries
That old man was on some elixir
Strychnine if lucky
I'm for it
If it'll toss me against walls
Just get me out of the heat
Before the floor melts away
Taking my feet in tow

Allegory of a Cultist

The world is on fire
Abruptly shaken awake
Crowds crash through streets
Hoping it will be their day
Weeks have gone into this
For some even months
All waiting for it to come to a boil
To overflow
And drag them all along
Towards the promises of another day

There are always stragglers
Ones who missed the point
Or revel in an oblivious paradise
A man can walk past the retching hordes
And hardly bat an eye
Those wind sailing messages
Those calming
Soothing tones
Are blocked off
No available entrance
They pass by
Searching for the willing host
Our subject will continue forward
Marching through their own separate existence
Permanent snapshots of scenery
Clouding visions
The pass over the new prevailing picture

Time has to pass before that change is noticed
Crowds disperse
All taken
Moved on
World in hand
When one cannot keep up
The earth itself falls away from feet
Plummet housing last seconds of ignorance
An otherwise blissful fall
The hit finally comes
Bringing an intensity
Almost indescribable in strength
Shaking awake

All rushing back
Faster at speeds
Until fog clears
And that true vision returns
Sparks of recreation fly
Allighting the flimsy facade previously held so dear
Their world becomes flame
And they can start to follow the trail

Yosemite

Mountain top
The high heaven
Sutras send us wandering
Past basins and wetlands
Up earth's steps
Searching for the peak
Both physical and mental
Brothers of the dharma scatter the way
Leading us onward
Upward
Wind pushes our backs forward
We march in harmony
With each other and the earth
The air thins
Awareness widens
Passing the fog
The valley is presented
Oaks and ferns reach high
Our feet far beyond their reach
Water flows
Seemingly directionless
Confused to its purpose
Before becoming one with gravity
And following its path
The chill sinks with each step
A breaking pain climbs throughout
We are solid
Like the rock
Move through unflinching
Moments from nirvana we reach a purpose
Discover the natural truth
Immense the ways with our own
A sheerfall make us weightless
Floating higher and higher
Collapsing
We see all
As clear as any picture
A world
Below us
Waits
We shall return
With the new knowledge

The high top aspirations
Freshly laden eyes and minds
Fear of the climb dissipates
Sends us home
To our brothers
Awaiting their climb

Decay and On the State of Things

A singer that refuses to sing is an artist
A runner that refuses to run is a genius
A man that refuses to learn is a fool
A crow that refuses to fly is an omen

Life and death interconnected
Inseparable
Existing only in tandem
Pointless apart
Those who know know peace
Those who don't die in vain
A man at peace changes the world
Divides it from reality
Moves along their own current
Far away from tricks and fools

Fools and kings
Kings and plagues
Despite well thought efforts
Men alike remain slaves
To a world
Designed to kill
Designed to benefit those with small hands
No thoughts
And bad haircuts

Art is dead
Freedom is dead
Life as we know it has expired
We must now create anew
Revive the fallen
Redesign life

(Untitled)

Demigod
Demilane
Demimore
Demigug

Look at me
Here I am
I am a
Demislug

Now I move
Slow as paste
Like cement
In the mud

With a face
Dark as snow
Falling free
Looking smug

Paisley Predetermined

Ick ick I am sick
Bruised and bent along the doorway
The fellas got jealous and sent me up town
Now I can't find my tongue
My hands are grey and numb
And the stars are falling upon me
So I'm cashing my check
That you rightfully owe
And claiming my right to the hallway

So she pulls out a coat
Old robe coloured green
Spreads it out on the floor

I pass back to a room
Yet she is there too
On the couch
With her feet
Far off on a table

With an escape to the kitchen
Throwing over pots
I lay my head on the counter
When I open my eyes
I've been dragged
To the floor
There she is
Sly look in one eye
And sleep in the other

I make a few calls
Tell them she has moved in
They're over with hands
Large arms
And a whistle
As she runs down the block
Trailing yellow and green
Shouts are all she has left me

The next day at my door
She says
My I am tired

Takes three boots
And a scarf
Shoots out for the beach
Then sails for the far lands of Persia

Lavender Pack Mule

The man had a fools gold tongue
Spreading
In appearance
The new calamitous gospel
The rancher had a scheme going
Some realists
Notably the professor
Say you only get three false truths per try
This shap-ed image
This mongrel
Was setting land speed records in terms
Three at a time on regular
In his down time the rate slowed
But hell
Politicians looked on in shame
Think of that
He had a certain philosophy for it
Some notable juxtapositions
Boiling down to a hatred for the alternative
When you can believe in anything you say
There's not a worry in the wave
Send in some doubt
The whole operation goes sideways
He always seemed more comfortable with the process
Who wouldn't be
Backers flock to it
Put feet to pavement
And carry the mindset on
Who needs an established truth
When the individual reigns supreme
When the quasi social enjoyment of it all acts as fuel

And he's leaving us in the grime

Mass Media Merging in the Meticulous Metropolitan Market

My land above
I just
What
No no no no no
We must shield this from polite company
We know what will happen
If even the slightest were to view such travesty
But just
How could this happen
So blatant
So
I shouldn't even describe
Don't we have systems
Or rule laden morals for such a situation
What's that?
We do?
Well then obviously we lack the operatives
As the facilities
If you are to be believed
Were intact and whole

Let's call blackout
Alert two and all the business
We've had drills for this
So let's jump into gear
I want a full temperamental recall
Cross axis scan shipped out
Feet off the floor by Monday
If we pass that threshold
We might have to go nuclear

No
Of course not
What do we even have to gain
Humanity is our mistress
And we must keep her sedated
Think of the prospective children
If you can
Their shattered cortexes littering the streets
We must work for them
Or abandon their hopes
Throw them behind

We can have no distractions on this
Allotted seconds have been collected
So time is non-negotiable
At least not in these circumstances
If we had the right incentives we might have something
Maybe we'll keep that avenue open
Keep it on the blackboard until further notice
In the chance we become advantageous
In the hypothetical future
Of course

(Untitled)

In the world we know
On a celebratory occasion
All bets
Thrown out
All floors
Thrown out
I will regard no regulations
They will not commend my will
A faint objective rush
Flash
Now he is one with the event
Entangled in his unwanted entrapment

Ah
Das ottoburg
Mein mind is in leashes
Now my feet move in patterns
Can I not fully understand what has passed
Shall I wonder with limited aim
A folly strikes that which sheds
For the sutras have spoken of actions before
Their eternal returning nature
I must relinquish all
Accept its payment in full truth
Act out the stone written example
But if fate seeks mistress
Then escape can be made
As fleet footed as any I make winds to follow
Turn tail
With the sullen brethren behind
Looking for life's real result
Though eyes can easily be diverted
Thoughts exchanged in time

Beaches

Hand draped over eye
Diving through water
With muck
Sludge evaporating
Escaping to capture breath
To regain life
Escaping to reach dry land
The otherside
Dry beaches
Where people of associations lie
Speak of dampened tongues
Music with frilled edges
Rampaging over ears
But moves without force
Now only a husk
Imitation of a beloved form

So now I must wander
Search
For solid
Unmoving ground
Ground with formed retention
There I will dig for gold
Find none
Yet claim answers were discovered
For that is the way
Which must never be discouraged

Das Poetique

What do you mean
I will not move because of your words
This is das poetique
You would never understand the motions
What is it you need
How you say
Feline comprehension
It isn't for all of us of course
Only us with toes in four sets
But
Why let that flatten your experience

(Untitled)

For I am here now
Where my feet lay
Promised that temperamental freedom
Preached by your masters
I have not found what is hidden
Yet I am here now
Proving not by how I speak
But remaining stalwart in composure
I will wait if needed
I will push if necessary
However
I can only retain this frame of mind for seconds
Minutes move
Every cell is thrown overboard
What sudden change overwhelms
Boiling like Liszt
Bursting in the exuberant cataclysm of expectation
Excited delirium tantamount
Free thinking
Omni-ambivolent movement
What have I become

Sonata for a Cock-Eyed Horse

We all live on pre-used tables
Life itself
The wealthy benefactor of eventual shift
Deemed the inexplicable standard
And how it rages
How it menaces all it claims
Allowing neither control
Nor illusion

I have spoken to my floors
The all hearing ears
And with wise lacquered tongue they spoke in return
My horror eternal
They spoke not
If so
I could not comprehend
Walls laughing in proxy disgrace
And with that
I was no longer in fair company
As all faith had evaporated
I maneuvered in escape

(Untitled)

Daughter mercy
Crawl faster forward
Grey cars come calling
Goodyear tires on holdaway
We must leave them in knee high ditches
Throw our past writings to their side
Take your two feet and climb
The deep tones have shaken loose
Our friends have sent word
Warring our masters upon arrival
As it was implied
We must follow
Keep eye for high birds
Dark wings of earth rock
We must never cross their path
Or we may never make our time

(Untitled)

When you fish for ill omens
Your eyes will be selectively blind
No comparison should be made
Unless weighing equal stone
And careful thought can be overturned
If corruption finds a weed

An analytical apocalypse will surface
Only when allowed to land
So mind all speech
It will only feed upon it
Proper tongue could be poison
Could flush them all into murky waters
Only with care
Only with care

Seekers of all Kinds

Then I will go to Penn State
Bullshit
And I will climb Everest
And I will find a golden box
And I
Of course
Will sit on my ass

I'm afflicted with realism
So these high flung images pass through
If I were to be a man of my word
My body would break
You would find my pieces in the street
Eaten as though before

But what a world you are denied
What life could you obtain
If only your corners were closer
They would never stop behind you
If you just knew where to step
It could all fall at your lap

And here we find that blatant sorrow
The kind we were promised
And I am sorrowful
For now my feet lack purpose
Withered
Died
And my legs will no longer support me
As they fear a shared fate
Woe is
Oh world of passing significance
Will you hear my plea and send me poor flowers
Show me how you grieve my living death
Or else move aside
And leave me to my own

Lyrics For Poet Mutts

1

I'm tired
And beat
And working sore
That is the life
Of a Broad Street whore

2

All those trees held golden leaves
Swaying back and forth
In the breeze from the window
Which transforms them
To thousands of golden voices
That fall in screaming melancholy
When the morning comes

3

Put on Monk
And die
To the world
That's all you ever need to know
It creates happiness
In spin
And when the world keeps spinning
Life moves on
And on
And on
Until we let it end

4

Most days
The morning brings the dog's bark
However many miles away
Whatever different life
The dog barks
In the morning
Shaken awake
By the sound and the sun
Or some hand
Just as warm

5

The brother was born
One hundred and twenty four years

To the day
But like others and so
He was mis-incarnated
So the world tried again
Once more
Seventeen would pass
After any a kid gets anxious
And when his time came
He was born
Billy the younger

6

Two old souls
Can't do much to stop a wave
They can let themselves be swallowed
Or they can step a ways back from the beach

7

If you're going to check on her
You may
As well
Take everything
She's got
That's just the kind of people we are

8

Id'd have shot a man in Reno
But I never found my gun
They left me seven bullets
And sent me on the run

9

Under Thursday's fog cover
I told her that I loved her
Though I'd said that to another
Yesterday

10

Oakland's always been my kind of town
It's where I go to lay my burdens down

11

I won't work for a suit and tie
If you know me
You know I'd die
If you don't know me
You should know why
I just won't work for a suit and tie

A suit and tie doesn't understand
The common plight
Of a common man
Their great big pockets
Hold great big hands
That grab and reach
For whatever they can

12

Like lovers
We longingly looked through the windows
Watching to see
If our life's soon to end

13

R. Bunnie Boone
Could eat skag all day
And bleed whenever he had to

14

That hard luck woman
From a hard luck town
Knew she wasn't kidding
Wasn't messing around
White cane line
Came to steal away my mind

Way down in Mississippi
Where you found me
You said baby
Come along with me
This white cane line

Will do anything you mind
This white cane line
Will do anything you mind
I'll be your girl
But I won't be your concubine

Left early in the morning
Way early in the day
Left me all strung up
Left me to pay
For the white cane line
Hell I'm sure that I'll be fine
White cane line
Hell I'm sure that I'll be fine
White cane line
All that's left of once was mine

15

God bless the dealers
And fine someone
To get their bail

16

I was born in Carson City to my mother
I first touched earth upon the kitchen floor
It took some time to see there was no other
My father left us both the week before

17

I need somebody to feed my baby
She gets so tired working out in the snow
I need somebody to feed my baby
She never quite cared
And that I know

18

There was a man who came to me
Who lived across that DMZ
Who sang so soft and poignantly
Though he died way back in '53

He was Korean born and so he seemed
When he came to me in that fever dream
Though he never spoke of things supreme
Those eyes held horrors that others had seen

He spoke of guns from either side
Strolled through valleys where children died
Never having taken a military stride
Caught in the center where worlds collide

19

You'll just have to believe me
It's not the time that grieves me
But the fact that I'm so far away from home

20

My legs are off
I've got the cough
My tongue is white as sin
The doctors say
You've been away
But we know where you've been
My hands were full
Of screaming dull
The curse was on my breath
Though I would bet
I won't hear yet
The coming call of death

In blackened sky
The birds will die
To never call my name
With trembling hand
My mother stands
I wish she'd do the same
Another day
Will come they say
Another day but one
With wordless eyes

I'll never spy
That ever rising sun

21

I've never been a betting man
Though when cards are right
I could be anything

22

Their names in ink
On pages sink
Into history's blackened tar
Destined to pass
From conscious mass
LIke an ancient dying star

23

I wandered far in the valley green
With clouds abound in the sky
So late that night I was not seen
As I wandered off to die

Five years on streets another land
I worked through day to night
While on home bred soil my heart did stand
In a sheltered land of light

24

When Jack comes over
Screaming
It's all I can do to say
Sorry
Je ne sprekenzie english
Amigo
And walk away sideways
As to not arouse suspicions

25

Some days I can't find the television
So I drink some more
And it all seems so normal
It all seems so fine

26

Let me live how I want
If it means I'll die by 25
Then that's how it will be
At least I can say
I did as much as I could to kill myself
Before the world did it for me

27

Have you seen Croatian skys
Have you seen Croatian women
Not all of them are nuns
Some of them you'll know longer
It's all about effort
For everyone
Whether you can pull her aside
Sing a hymn
And change your traditional uniform
I've always wanted Croatian girls
Or any girls
Who will let me settle for a drink**28**
I'm not warm
Cause she's not warm
So I'm not warm
Cause she's not warm
So I just lay there beside her
Awake
I won't sleep
Until I'm warm
Though I'm used to it
So not sleeping tonight
Will hardly keep me down
As far as I'm awake
She's still not warm

29

I've been to Boston
Where the sweet girls sing

For the preacher
Who makes the church bells ring
For the birds bees bruins
Damn near anything
Where a calm cool kid could even claim he's a king

30

I'm a rolling stone
And I ain't seen water
For a day or more
I've been born to wander
Through those dying hills
Lying way out yonder
I'm a rolling stone
In a Barstow brothel
Caught the Barstow blues
Those Barstow women
All I ever knew
They'd always ask me
Honey what'll you do
I'm a rolling stone

31

I knew a girl
Her name was Trish
She would only eat
Kafildafish
That fish went rotten
She had to blow
Whether she's alright
I just don't know

32

Let me know if I'm wrong
But it'd do some good to hear one last song
Before they drop that atom bomb

33

Behind my bedside
I heard the thousand voices
Of all the women and children
Screaming
Who had to watch those they trust
Walk away to the wilderness
Stoic or unrelenting
Deaf and dumb to the world
And all around them

34

Killer of women
Killer of men
They say he's killed seven
They say he's killed ten
I've killed more
As everyone has
Quietly
Behind our walls
So if he can't match what we demand
He'll be as useless to us
As anything else
Killer of women
Killer of men
If he knows what's best
Then he'll kill again

35

Jesus Christ is a scab
But hell
I don't even know who that is

36

I'm snorting snakes
Like they're candy cigarettes
So when my head
Goes up in smoke
Only the odd onlooker
Walks away surprised

37

I want a president
With no teeth
So they can't fake a smile

38

My daughter
Would keep her arms
Held close to his chest

39

There's no sense living
When you're twenty one
And never took your first breath

40

South Florida floods
Will wash me away
I know it's true
Of course it's true

41

Why can't the elephants pay the bills
Why can't the elephants pay the bills
They tear down the alleyways
And stomp down the hills
So why can't the elephants pay the bills

42

I want fair representation
In my elation
I just want to avoid
Annihilation
But this nation
Of mass migration
Can't help but feel some indignation

43

I won't throw blame
When there's fire in the air
And our hands are burnt

44

I wanted to write haiku
Like the Japanese masters
But I failed

45

Liam oh Liam is scared of the hail
A nose to warm climates
Is how he will sail
But he'll start to shiver
As winds bring the gails

Jesus oh Jesus
Well he had a son
They say his name's Michael
They say he's the one
Looking back now
Can't say what he's done

Save me oh save me
Calls Lima so cold
The sky's growing evil
And screaming so bold
This is not the place
For young or the old

As they carried Michael
They came up to me
They spoke of his favour
I could not agree
But they would not listen
And I would not see

46

If you really insist
I'll be off it tomorrow
Just give me a day
To finish what I've got

47

Burn the rich with napalm gas
And plant a tree
Where their houses stood

48

I cannot see the world
For I am of the world
And the world has no eyes